Honoring Yosemite's Unsung Hero

After *Sierra Heritage* Magazine featured a story on "Yosemite's Unsung Hero," Congress and the National Parks Promotion Council honored the role Jessie Benton Fremont had in the first effort to save Yosemite. Following are excerpts from each tribute:

From a Speech by Hon. Jeff Denham of California in the House of Representatives on March 20, 2012 (Congressional Record): "Mr. Speaker, I rise today during Women's History Month to honor the life and legacy of Jessie Benton Fremont, who helped inspire and lead efforts to preserve and protect what is now a very significant part of Yosemite National Park.... Please join me in posthumously honoring Jessie for her unwavering leadership and activism to preserve the beauty and grandeur of Yosemite Valley for generations to come. Her legacy serves as an example of excellence, and her accomplishments and contributions to Yosemite National Park will never be forgotten."

From the National Parks Promotion Council's March 21st Newsletter: "...Often the influence of women in parks has been overlooked because during the era when parks were established, women did not have a vote or were not in positions where their actions were on the public record....Historian Craig MacDonald asked recently, "If not for what she did behind the scene, would there be a Yosemite National Park today, would John Muir have been drawn to the valley because of the attention given it by its protection, would there even have been the foundation necessary to lead to establishing national parks?'...."

On March 14, 2013, Congressman Tom McClintock introduced a Bill (HR 1192) in the House of Representatives "to redesignate Mammoth Peak in Yosemite National Park as 'Mount Jessie Benton Fremont,' to be known informally as 'Mt. Jessie,' recognizing Jessie's efforts to preserve Yosemite for future generations through the Yosemite Grant, signed by President Lincoln on June 30, 1864. This was the first time land was set aside for its preservation and public use by a national government and set the foundation for the creation of national and state parks through her advocacy for and influence on the Yosemite Grant." On July 14, 2014, The House of Representatives passed HR1192 and sent it to the Senate.

YOSEMITE'S UNSUNG HERO

By Craig MacDonald

Illustrated by **Bill Anderson**

Special Painting of Half Dome by **Milford Zornes**

Mesa Art Publishing
789 W. 19th St. Costa Mesa, CA. 92627
e-mail: frank@mesaart.net
Available Art Reproductions at: www.billandersonartist.com

DEDICATED to **JESSIE BENTON FREMONT** and her friends, who successfully helped save Yosemite Valley and the Mariposa Grove of Giant Sequoias (36 miles south of the valley). Jessie passed away 110 years ago.

DEDICATED to **SIERRA HERITAGE** Magazine for keeping the history of the Sierra Alive. Two of my articles on Jessie appeared in this beautiful, full-color publication that also tells all you can do throughout the Sierra and features sensational photos & artwork. Find out more at www.sierraheritage.com

Pulitzer Prize Nominee **Craig MacDonald**, a member of Phi Alpha Theta, the national history honor society, is the author of 18 books on the West. His grandfather, C.E. Curry, was a friend of David and Jennie Curry, who created Camp Curry at Yosemite. The historian also is a professional speaker. Read more about his books and how to hire him for your conference at www.goldrushglimpses.com. Email: ccmacdo@yahoo.com

Bill Anderson, who loves to paint Yosemite, has artwork hanging in museums and galleries around the world. The award-winning watercolor painter's gallery is at 16812 Pacific Coast Highway, Sunset Beach, Ca. Email: aagcollection@aol.com. Website: www.billandersonartgallery.com

Table of Contents

Image 001

Image 002

Jessie Benton Fremont

YOSEMITE'S UNSUNG HERO

Jessie Benton Fremont fell in love with Yosemite the very first time she saw it in the late 1850s. She had recently moved to California from back east and was totally awestruck with the unparalleled beautiful grandeur of the place. But she also was gravely concerned by what was starting to happen to this most spectacular scenery.

The wife of Explorer John C. Fremont envisioned settlers homesteading, orchards being planted, cattle and sheep overgrazing, loggers sawing down giant sequoias and wildlife being killed for fun.

Jessie was determined to preserve and protect Yosemite and she did something about it. She gathered friends and others together in her homes at Bear Valley, near Mariposa (1858-59), and Black Point, overlooking the Golden Gate in San Francisco (1860-61).

She and her guests regularly discussed how to save Yosemite at afternoon teas and Sunday dinners. Jessie wrote a friend describing her 1-3 hour teas as "delightful and chatty." Everyone at her teas and dinners had something to contribute.

Among her guests were writers like Bret Harte, Herman Melville, Richard Henry Dana, Jr. and famous New York journalist, Horace Greeley.

Other friends, who enjoyed her hospitality, took prominent roles in the first effort to save Yosemite, including Orator/Writer/Minister Thomas Starr King, Photographer Carleton Watkins, Businessman Israel Ward Raymond and Geologists Josiah D. Whitney and William Ashburner. Mountaineer Galen Clark also met with her on occasion.

Effervescent Jessie inspired and encouraged her distinguished pals to lobby Congress, the media and acquaintances on the immediate need to preserve Yosemite Valley and the Mariposa Grove of Giant Sequoias, before it's too late.

Jessie loved working behind the scenes, never desiring any credit for her role in orchestrating the first effort to save Yosemite. She preferred bringing people together, introducing them and planting her brilliant ideas in the minds of influential men.

An excited Thomas Starr King wrote Randolph Ryers, on Oct. 29, 1860:
"I am going to dine today at Mrs. Fremonts (Black Point) with Colonel Baker, the new Republican Senator from Oregon." Baker was a good friend of Abraham Lincoln and helped spread the gospel for saving Yosemite Valley. He was just one of the politicians she invited to her friendly gatherings.

"Jessie's role was that of a catalyst and muse, prodding and encouraging (them) to write and speak," wrote John Henneberger of the National Park Service.

Her house guests appreciated her advice and passion. Jessie knew what she was talking about. She was taught how to bring "the right" people together and lobby Congress and even Presidents by her father, Thomas Hart Benton, once the most powerful U.S. Senator in Washington.

"Jessie is sublime and carries guns enough to be formidable to a whole cabinet," wrote Thomas Starr King to a friend. "She's thoroughly sheathed and carrying fire in the genuine Benton furnace."

Conversations in her homes sparked interest in early conservation efforts that impacted King and others. He visited Yosemite in July of 1860, calling it, "The grandest piece of rock and water scenery in the world." The enthusiastic preacher saw it as another "magnificent revelation of God's eternal glory."
He emotionally preached about it upon his return to San Francisco.
(Josiah D. Whitney, who later became a Yosemite Park Commissioner, attended King's Unitarian Church.)

Jessie even provided space in her Black Point residence for King to write sermons, lectures and newspaper articles for papers like the *Boston Evening Transcript*. He had planned on doing a story on Yosemite but was so taken by its splendor that he ended up creating eight Yosemite pieces for the Boston paper between Dec. 1, 1860 and Feb. 9, 1861.

In one descriptive column, he raved about a horseback trip through Yosemite Valley, declaring: "Is there such a ride possible in any other part of the planet?" His passionate contributions helped gain, not only public, but future Congressional support for preservation efforts. He continued to visit Yosemite and the Sierra and preach as well as write about its incredible beauty.

Richard Henry Dana, Jr., famous for his book, *Two Years Before the Mast*, visited Jessie at her Bear Valley home in August of 1859 and toured Yosemite Valley and the Big Trees. He wrote "Yosemite Valley was a stupendous miracle of nature" and called Mrs. Fremont, "a heroine…"

Also in 1859, Jessie invited famous journalist Horace Greeley to stay at the Fremont's Bear Valley home and visit Yosemite and the giant sequoias for the first time. He wrote in the *New York Tribune*, "Yosemite is the grandest marvel of the continent….Nothing else dwells in my memory that's at all comparable in awe-inspiring grandeur."

He loved the giant sequoias and pleaded on their behalf: "If the …county or state does not immediately provide for the safety of them, I shall deeply deplore it…. I'm sure they will be more prized and treasured a thousand years from now… should they be preserved so long." Greeley continued to write more on Yosemite and encourage its preservation.

On several occasions, Jessie met with President Abraham Lincoln to discuss subjects, including saving Yosemite. In 1862, she and her husband joined the President and some cabinet members on the Smithsonian Institution stage, where Horace Greeley gave a lecture. She then threw a reception at her hotel for the President and Greeley.

Noted Landscape Architect Frederick Law Olmsted, who designed New York's Central Park, came to California in 1863 to manage Rancho Las Mariposas and fell in love with Yosemite. He called it, "the greatest glory of nature" and the giant sequoias as "the grandest tall trees you ever saw." Olmsted was friends with the Fremonts and joined in the preservation effort to save Yosemite Valley and the Mariposa Grove.

Meanwhile, Carleton Watkins, who met Thomas Starr King and Israel Ward Raymond at her get-togethers, created the most extensive and impressive photographic record of Yosemite. His spectacular images brought the area's awe to the nation (in magazines, newspapers and gallery exhibits) and later the world (at the Paris International Exposition).

In 1864, through Jessie's encouragement, Israel Ward Raymond sent some of Watkins' sensational pictures and a letter to U.S. Senator John Conness of California asking him to create a bill to save Yosemite Valley and the Mariposa Grove of Giant Sequoias. Conness reportedly shared the awesome photos with others in Congress as well as with the President. These pictures helped seal the deal.

"I think it's important to obtain the proprietorship soon to preserve the trees in the valley from destruction and ....to give Commissioners power to take control and begin laying out plans for the gradual improvement of the properties," Raymond wrote Conness. These two special areas, "...should be granted for public use, resort and recreation and be inalienable forever...."

Sen. Conness had the bill drawn up and encouraged its passage. Jessie, King, Raymond, Olmsted and others also lobbied for the bill. On June 30, 1864, President Lincoln signed an Act of Congress giving the Yosemite Valley and Mariposa Grove of Giant Sequoias to the State of California "...for public use, resort and recreation and be inalienable forever...."

This reportedly was the first time in the world that any national government set aside scenic land, protecting it for future generations. It marked the beginning of the state and national park movement in the United States.

Enthusiastic Jessie was "the link," who with her friends, helped make it happen, four years before John Muir came to Yosemite for the first time.

Galen Clark, who was selected the first official Guardian of Yosemite, later wrote, "Jessie and Raymond were the most active workers on the Yosemite Park Proposal."

The Yosemite Grant set aside 36,111 acres of Yosemite Valley and 2,500 acres containing the Mariposa Grove of Big Trees to be "entrusted to the State of California" and managed by 8 Commissioners.

Several of Jessie's friends were on the Commission, including Frederick Law Olmsted, Israel Ward Raymond, Galen Clark, William Ashburner and Josiah D. Whitney.

Her tea and/or dinner guests and other friends have prominent sites named for them at Yosemite, including:

--**Mount Starr Point,** south of Nevada Fall, is named for Thomas Starr King. A meadow east of this point also is named in his honor.

--**Mount Raymond** in Madera County is named for Israel Ward Raymond.

--**Olmsted Point** near Tenaya Lake is named for Frederick Law Olmsted (and his son, Frederick Law Olmsted, Jr., who was on the Yosemite Board of Expert Advisors from 1928-56).

--**Mount Watkins**, whose reflection is seen in Mirror Lake, is named for Carleton Watkins.

--**Clark Point,** on the south side of Merced Canyon, near Vernal Fall, is named for Galen Clark. There's also the Galen Clark Tree, in the Mariposa Grove of Giant Sequoias.

--**Mount Conness**, west of Hale Natural Area on the border of Yosemite and Inyo National Parks, is named for U.S. Senator John Conness, R-California. He knew Jessie and her husband John, who had been a U.S. Senator and the Republican Party's first candidate for President of the United States.

(For all her efforts in being the longtime catalyst and encourager of Yosemite's Preservation, it's this historian's belief that there should be a Point, Peak, River, Mountain, Meadow, Path or Tree named in honor of Jessie Benton Fremont. She was the thread that wove the preservation effort, that brought the people together, that did everything possible to make it happen, without ever seeking any type of credit. She was a true patriot for preservation, who only wanted one thing—to save Yosemite Valley and the Mariposa Grove of Giant Sequoias.)

Even after the record-setting Yosemite Grant, Jessie and her friends continued to promote the beauty and preservation of the area all their lives.

In 1868, four years after the grant, John Muir, who would become Yosemite's most famous resident and "savior," visited the nation's first park for the first time. He would passionately document "the soul" of Yosemite and start a successful campaign, with *Century Magazine* Editor Robert Underwood Johnson, to establish Yosemite National Park, protecting the area outside the Yosemite Grant territory, including some valuable meadows and the high country region.

On October 1, 1890, the United States Government enacted the law that established Yosemite National Park, setting aside 1,500 square miles of land.

With state and national Yosemite Parks next to each other, there was overlap and conflict, leading to the state returning Yosemite Valley and the Mariposa Grove to the federal government to be included in Yosemite National Park.

Unfortunately, Jessie did not live to see it. She died on Dec. 27, 1902, less than 4 years before it happened. In her obituary, *The Los Angeles Times* described her as "brilliant and beautiful... now only a memory is left of her wit, her gracious use of power, her influence for good...."

Image 003

SOME WHO HELPED JESSIE SAVE THE VALLEY AND GROVE

President Lincoln

Sen. John Conness

Thomas Starr King

Horace Greeley

Carleton Watkins

Frederick Law Olmsted

Galen Clark

YOSEMITE VALLEY

Image 004

Image 005

Image 006

Image 007

MILFORD ZORNES (1908-2008)

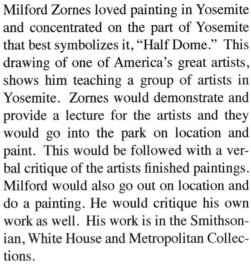

Milford Zornes loved painting in Yosemite and concentrated on the part of Yosemite that best symbolizes it, "Half Dome." This drawing of one of America's great artists, shows him teaching a group of artists in Yosemite. Zornes would demonstrate and provide a lecture for the artists and they would go into the park on location and paint. This would be followed with a verbal critique of the artists finished paintings. Milford would also go out on location and do a painting. He would critique his own work as well. His work is in the Smithsonian, White House and Metropolitan Collections.

Drawing by Bill Anderson, who assisted Milford at this workshop and many others as well.

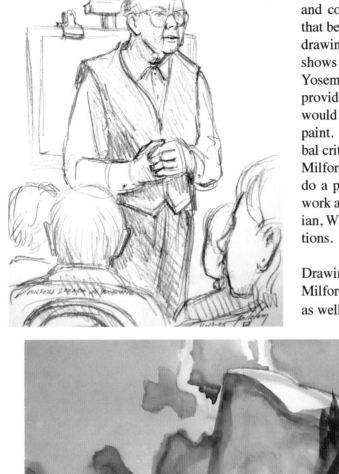

Image 008

"Half Dome" Watercolor by Milford Zornes

16

Image 009

Image 010

"YOSEMITE"

Image 011

Image 012

Image 013

Image 014

Image 015

Image 016

Image 019

Image 20

Image 021

Mammoth Peak on the Northern end of Yosemite National Park's Kuna Crest (near California State Route 120) may be renamed "Mount Jessie Benton Fremont." The House National Resources Committee approved HR1192 to redesignate the 12,117-foot peak and sent the bill to the House for a vote. Senate approvals also are needed.

150 years ago, the efforts of Jessie Benton Fremont and her friends helped save spectacular Yosemite Valley (and what became the Mariposa Grove of Giant Sequoias) when President Abraham Lincoln signed the Yosemite Grant Act on June 30, 1864. This was the first time a federal government saved scenic lands for the future generations and it led to the national park movement. If they haden't done this, there may not be a Yosemite National Park today.

Artist Bill Anderson

Image 017

Mariposa Grove of Giant Sequoias

MORE ON JESSIE

This Century, there has been a lot of talk about a woman running for President. But more than 150 years ago, there were many in the United States, who thought a female would actually be in the White House, running the country.

The amazing individual, who resided on-and-off in California for more than 50 years, was Jessie Benton Fremont. In 1856, the incredible wife of the first Republican Party candidate for President, John C. Fremont, was so dynamic that wherever she went, crowds shouted fervently, "Jessie, Jessie, Jessie." They waived signs, "Jessie for the White House" and "Fremont and Jessie, too!" (This was 64 years before all women got the right to vote in the 19th Amendment!)

Even the Democrats repeatedly told the media and public that Jessie was the real candidate; the one who wore the pants in the family; the one who would really run the country, if her husband was elected. And, they were probably right.

Jessie definitely knew politics inside and out as the daughter, secretary and confidant of powerful Democratic U.S. Senator Thomas Hart Benton of Missouri. She helped her father prepare speeches, represented him at some events and acted as hostess at his political gatherings. She even went with her dad to talk with Presidents Andrew Jackson and Martin Van Buren in the White House. She knew all the political players in Congress. She was a brilliant thinker, writer, promoter and lobbyist.

Many in America, including the media, also called the Fremonts, "the most glamorous couple in the country."

Historians say the articulate-speaking, raven-haired beauty was the first wife in American History to play such an active role in a Presidential Bid.

With vigor, she took control of her husband's campaign—reviewing and answering much of his correspondence; writing his dynamic speeches, campaign literature and even a biography. One professor said, "Fremont acquired by marriage, a very attractive literary style."

Even future President Abe Lincoln was impressed by Jessie's abundant talent, telling her, "You're quite a female politician."

And, she almost made it to the White House but her husband's lack of political experience (only 6 months as a U.S. Senator) and her own father's campaigning for long-time Democratic Senator/Representative James Buchanan, didn't help matters. (Ironically, Jessie had translated documents in Spanish and French for Buchanan, when he was Secretary of State.)

Why Senator Benton "turned" on his son-in-law and daughter is a story in itself—partly about supporting a fellow Democrat and partly a lingering bitterness towards Fremont.

Benton reportedly brought 16-year-old Jessie along with him to a U.S. Army mapping meeting, where she met Fremont. Some say the handsome lieutenant, 10 years her senior, first met Jessie at the Benton home, when he visited the senator to talk about Western Exploration. Jessie was smitten with the dashing gent and, when her father noticed the mutual infatuation, he forbade her to see Fremont. Instead, she smuggled letters to him and when he returned from a journey, they eloped to Washington, D.C. and got married on Oct. 19, 1841. The senator was furious.

What she had done, took a lot of guts, and 15 years later, she and her husband still had guts, pushing for what they thought was necessary. They were dead set against slavery and did all they could to abolish it during the campaign and for the rest of their lives. Unfortunately for the Fremonts, they were ahead of their time.

Buchanan won the election but they did make it to a "white house," one in Bear Valley, 12 miles northwest of Mariposa, Ca.

The home was built on land purchased for Fremont by a proxy prior to the Gold Discovery. It was known as the "Mariposas Tract," a floating land grant, whose borders could expand for cattle grazing and other things. When gold was discovered, the borders did expand until the 70-square-mile property included gold mines. Fremont leased out some of his mines but there was much costly and lengthy litigation over land rights.

The vivacious Jessie was a charming hostess and got along great with many of her neighbors, whom she invited over to enjoy the home's marble-topped furniture and piano. (Some of her furniture and other belongings are on display at the Mariposa Museum and History Center, 5119 Jessie St., named in her honor. Also, Jessie came up with the name "May Rock," 2 miles southeast of Bear Valley, where she had a delightful May picnic.)

Edward Bosqui, who managed some of Fremont's mine holdings, called Jessie, "a highly accomplished woman of fine intellect with towering ambition and courage equal to her husbands."

She absolutely fell in love with the Sierra, especially Yosemite Valley and, what would become known as "the Mariposa Grove of Giant Sequoias." On one camping trip, she was in awe "of the grandeur of the silent forest…trees eight-feet in diameter, rising straight as masts over 100-feet, the golden green canopy through which, high, high above, only a mist of sunlight came, made a cathedral dignity that hushed us."

She not only shared her excitement for it with others, she made a commitment to preserve the grove and valley, bringing friends together on a regular basis, first at her Bear Valley residence, then San Francisco home, to make it happen.

Jessie loved California, but with a Civil War "brewing," the Fremonts moved to St. Louis, where John was appointed Army General and Commander of the Western Region.

While assisting her husband in his duties, she kept lobbying to save Yosemite. She met with President Lincoln on several occasions trying to passionately bring about an end to slavery and to save Yosemite. In 1864, the President signed the bill granting Yosemite Valley and the Mariposa Grove to the state as an inalienable public trust.

Later, the Fremonts returned to California and fell on hard times. Squatters had taken gold from some of their property and John lost a fortune in a major railroad venture which did not "pan out." He made some other bad business decisions, too.

But Jessie was there to come to the rescue. Just as she had helped him write his acclaimed books and reports on Western Exploration, she again stepped forward with her pen and started supporting the family by writing about fascinating people and places.

Harpers Magazine, Atlantic Monthly and other publications were eager for her "inside" stories, especially about Washington, D.C. and the Sierra. (She later had several popular books published, including *A Year of American Travel*, *Souvenirs of My Time*, *Memoirs of My Life*, and *Far West Sketches*. The last one wonderfully describes her adventures in the Sierra and her appreciation of nature.)

Meanwhile, John became sick and doctors told him to move to a warmer climate. So, they went to Los Angeles, where his health improved. However, on a trip to New York, the 77-year-old man known as "The Pathfinder," got very ill and told his doctors he wanted to return home to Jessie in Los Angeles. He never got the chance.

On July 13, 1890, he died in New York. Jessie remained active, continued to write and was much admired and respected by her many friends. She was made Honorary First Regent for the Daughters of the American Revolution's Los Angeles Chapter. Several prominent figures came to visit her, including President William McKinley.

Throughout her married life, Jessie had an unwavering loyalty and love for her husband—through good times and bad. Her intelligence, positive attitude and enthusiastic passion not only made her a fantastic spouse (and mother of five) but she undoubtedly could have run the country, just like her supporters had thought.

This captivating, caring, remarkable lady, so full of guts and gumption, quietly left her mark on the country.

She once proudly said that from the ashes of her husband's campfires, sprung cities. But it also can be said that from Jessie's passion, sprung the first efforts to help preserve Yosemite, so it can be enjoyed forever! These initial efforts inspired others, leading to our nation's state and national parks.

THE IMPORTANCE OF PRESERVING PARKS

Frederick Law Olmsted's 1865 Preliminary Report on Yosemite and the Mariposa Grove shows "the importance of contact with wilderness for human well-being, the effects of beautiful scenery on human perception, and the moral responsibility of democratic governments to preserve regions of extraordinary natural beauty for the benefit of the whole people."

--Library of Congress' American Memory on "The Evolution of the Conservation Movement, 1850-1920"

"Climb the mountains and get their good tidings. Nature's peace will flow into you as sunshine flows into trees. The winds will blow their own freshness into you, and the storms their energy, while cares will drop off like Autumn leaves."

--John Muir

John Muir

--"We simply need that wild country available to us, even if we never do more than drive to its edge and look in...." --*Wallace Stegner*

--"Glimpses of Yosemite Valley in the morning freshness made us glad we were alive." --*Jessie Benton Fremont*

Fascinating Footnote: Famous American Painter and Muralist Thomas Hart Benton was named after his great-uncle, Jessie's father. In 1939, he named his own daughter, Jessie Benton, after Yosemite's Unsung Hero.

Image 018

Art Reproductions Available
Giclee Prints of Original
Watercolors
Acid free paper
Archival inks

Order at:
www.billandersonartist.com
Contact:
e-mail: frank@mesaart.net
(949) 548-3570